Horse Racing the Statistical Route Four

Purely Odds-Starting Prices Sp's of Horses

A Statistical Study of the Starting Prices of Horse Races

These are a look at the percentage rate of the odds horses win and get placed for individual types of races. Where are the odds-on horses coming in, where are the 16/1 shots more likely to fall etc.

2774 races were looked at, less for jumps than flat. 666 jump races, 449 all weather races and 1659 flat races. These were divided into handicaps and non handicaps plus further divided into 4-7 runners, 8-11 runners, 12-15 runners and 16+ runners.

The book contains tables showing the results of this for wins and placed. In the example below for Handicap All Weather Races for 12-15 runners the first column represents the odds, the next three columns show the amount of times horses of those odds came 1st, 2nd and 3rd. The 5th column the total and the 6th column the percentage arranged to show the highest percentages first. So the first line shows that horses of 4/1+ won 10, came 2nd 12 times, came 3rd 10 times, a total of 32 representing 40 % of the races analysed which is in brackets.

Han All Weather 12-15 runners (80)

odds	1st	2nd	3rd	total	%
4+	10	12	10	32	40.00
3+	11	9	4	24	30.00
5+	11	6	7	24	30.00
17+	3	6	13	22	27.50
8+	5	8	8	21	26.25
6+	4	8	5	17	21.25
7+	4	4	7	15	18.75
16+	6	3	6	15	18.75

The book further sorts a lot of this information into top 10 and top 20 results in various ways.

The book may be useful to show horses you're interested in, depending on what the odds are, if it is a type of race where horses of those odds do well or not as the case may be. However, I must stress this is not a guaranteed way to make money but a helpful guide nevertheless and may help in your overall strategy.

Compiler-Mark Gaster

First Published 2016

© MG Internet Publishing

ABOUT THE BOOK

To be honest these odds statistics were taken when compiling statistics as part of another book. This will be book 5 in the series just based on race card numbers. This book was going to be part of that however, I realised this would become too much, Books with too many statistics and tables can be a bit too much to absorb so I decided there was just enough to make these odds statistics a book in its own right. And better two cheaper smaller books of this type that's easier to absorb than one bigger book covering both themes.

There are some considerations with these odds; they were the SP price results the horses came in at after the race. Of course these can vary before a race so it does present some difficulty when comparing the tables in this book on the day before a race starts. Also they are not a true statistic in one sense because it was not noted for example just how many say 5 / 1 horses were on offer in a race before the off. This would vary from race to race whatever odds were on offer, be it 10/1, 2/1 etc.

Still, when you look further into the book I think you will glean some help from it. The propensity for some odds to succeed or fail does show a variation in different types of races, some are better for long shots and some are better for very short priced horses for example. This may be of help as part of an overall strategy. This is of course up to you how you use this book; my job is just to show the results. It takes time to collect them and formulate them into coherent tables and this is what I have done. They are there then for anyone who thinks they might be interesting or helpful in some way.

THE BOOK LAYOUT

I have divided the races into 8 types and 4 sizes of runners. They are

- handicap hurdles,
- non handicap hurdles
- handicap chases
- non handicap chases,
- handicap all weather
- non handicap all weather
- handicap flat
- non handicap flat

In all cases these were further divided into

- 4-7 runners
- 8-11 runners
- 12-15 runners
- 16+ runners.

The odds are shown as **0+** which denotes all horses of odds below 1/1, **1+** which denotes all horses of 1 but below 2, **2+**, and **3+** and so on. In fact it was set up as 2 to 2.99 and 3 to 3.99 and so on. Up to 16+ (16 to 16.99) and the last odds category which was 17+; these were all horses of 17/1 and over. Below is a table giving a bit more information for clarity.

0+	Odds on 0 to.99
1+	Odds 1 to 1.99
2+	Odds 2 to 2.99
3+	Odds 3 to 3.99
4+	Odds 4 to 4.99
5+	"
6+	"
7+	"
8+	"
9+	"
10+	"
11+	"
12+	"
13+	"
14+	"
15+	"
16+	Odds 16 to 16.99
17+	All odds 17 and over

In practice most returned odds are similar, usually even numbers at the higher end, 8/1 10/1 12/1 etc. 13's 15's are rare so take this into account when looking at the results.

The first part of the book shows the results for 1st, 2nd and 3rd added together and then shown as a percentage to the total number of races analysed. For example in the table below in Handicap All Weather races of 12 to 15 runners; horses of odds of 4/1 but below 5/1 came first 10 times, 2nd 12 times and 3rd 10 times. This gives a total of 32; 80 races were analysed making 100/80*32 which equals 40%.

Han All Weather 12-15 runners (80)

odds	1st	2nd	3rd	total	%
4+	10	12	10	32	40.00

All the tables are laid out like this, at the top showing the type of race, the number of runners and in brackets the number of races analysed.

In the second part of the book the tables are laid out the same but for win only figures. In the same example below horses of 4/1 but below 5/1 came 1st 10 times giving 100/80*10 which equal 12.5%:-

Han All Weather 12-15 runners (80)

odds	1st	%
4+	10	12.5

PLEASE NOTE in some cases for the sake of space I have used the following abbreviations. This only occurs when I compiled the top ten and twenty tables at the end of each section of the book for example:-

hh1 = handicap hurdle race 4-7 runners

hh2 = handicap hurdle race 8=11 runners.

hh3 = handicap hurdle race 12-15 runners

And so on. hch = handicap chases, naw = non handicap all weather races etc etc. Plus 1, 2, 3, and 4 denote 4-7, 8-11, 12-15 and 16+ runners respectively.

This will be easier to spot once you have got used to the book.

PLEASE ALSO NOTE some race types are missing from the statistics, there were just not enough statistics of some race types to include in the book; mostly the big runner fields of 16+ runners. My line drawn was at least 20 incidents to include in the book although in the case of non handicap flat races of 16+ runners there were 19 so I allowed that in.

NOTE: - Non Runners

If for example an 8 horse race had a non runner in it, then it was still an 8 horse race for the purposes of these statistics. However, if any race had more than one non runner I did not take the statistic down for that race. I felt more than one non runner would upset the balance too much. This does mean in some cases an 8 runner race would only produce a 1st and 2nd result. This does not affect the tables in any way but, you may notice some discrepancy in the totals for the statistics, this is why.

JUST A WARNING ABOUT STATISTICS

A lot of people mistrust statistics and I can understand why. They can manipulate them to prove a point or if they have an axe to grind. It's not always dishonest; they just only print statistics that prove their point and leave out any that do not. I would just like to stress, I have no point to prove or axe to grind. I give you the results exactly as they turned out.

However, words of warning, statistics are a lesson in history, they can educate and enable us to form a better judgement but there is not a guarantee they will replicate themselves. Please be careful, it's not my job to advise you where and how to invest your money; that's a decision for you to make, I can only give you the results of this study and hopefully you will find them useful or educational. But, please be careful, do not get carried away, test the water by all means and only gamble what you can afford.

WHERE THE ODDS FALL WIN AND PLACED

Hopefully you would have read the previous chapter and be familiar with how the tables in this section are laid out. Each table heading shows the type of race, number of runners and in brackets the number of races analysed. The first column the odds, the next three columns how often horses came in at those odds 1st, 2nd and 3rd. The fourth column the total and the fifth column that total realized as a percentage against the number of races analysed.

Han Hurdles 4-7 runners (50)

odds	1st	2nd	3rd	total	%
2+	13	7	0	20	40.00
3+	5	10	0	15	30.00
1+	6	7	0	13	26.00
4+	7	5	0	12	24.00
5+	5	3	0	8	16.00
7+	2	5	0	7	14.00
8+	2	3	0	5	10.00
6+	3	1	0	4	8.00
0+	3	0	0	3	6.00
16+	0	3	0	3	6.00
17+	0	3	0	3	6.00
12+	1	1	0	2	4.00
14+	1	1	0	2	4.00
9+	1	0	0	1	2.00
10+	1	0	0	1	2.00
11+	0	0	0	0	0.00
13+	0	0	0	0	0.00
15+	0	0	0	0	0.00

Han Hurdles 8-11 runners (134)

odds	1st	2nd	3rd	total	%
2+	18	15	15	48	35.82
3+	20	18	10	48	35.82
4+	17	16	13	46	34.33
5+	16	14	9	39	29.10
7+	8	12	12	32	23.88
17+	4	6	17	27	20.15
8+	6	8	12	26	19.40
6+	12	11	2	25	18.66
1+	11	8	5	24	17.91
10+	5	7	7	19	14.18
12+	6	5	8	19	14.18
9+	3	4	6	13	9.70
14+	2	5	2	9	6.72
16+	1	3	4	8	5.97
0+	5	0	0	5	3.73
11+	0	2	0	2	1.49
13+	0	0	0	0	0.00
15+	0	0	0	0	0.00

Han Hurdles 12-15 runners (54)

odds	1st	2nd	3rd	total	%
4+	3	11	3	17	31.48
16+	6	2	7	15	27.78
17+	3	7	5	15	27.78
5+	4	1	9	14	25.93
7+	3	5	6	14	25.93
2+	6	5	2	13	24.07
8+	4	2	7	13	24.07
9+	7	4	2	13	24.07
6+	4	4	3	11	20.37
3+	6	4	0	10	18.52
14+	1	2	5	8	14.81
12+	3	1	3	7	12.96
10+	0	5	0	5	9.26
11+	2	1	2	5	9.26
1+	2	0	0	2	3.70
0+	0	0	0	0	0.00
13+	0	0	0	0	0.00
15+	0	0	0	0	0.00

Non Han Hurdles 4-7 runners (69)

odds	1st	2nd	3rd	total	%
0+	22	9	0	31	44.93
2+	15	13	0	28	40.58
1+	13	10	0	23	33.33
3+	5	5	0	10	14.49
17+	2	6	0	8	11.59
4+	5	2	0	7	10.14
8+	1	2	0	3	4.35
10+	2	1	0	3	4.35
16+	0	3	0	3	4.35
5+	1	1	0	2	2.90
6+	0	2	0	2	2.90
7+	0	2	0	2	2.90
12+	1	0	1	2	2.90
14+	0	2	0	2	2.90
9+	1	0	0	1	1.45
11+	1	0	0	1	1.45
13+	0	0	0	0	0.00
15+	0	0	0	0	0.00

Non Han Hurdles 8-11 runners (89)

odds	1st	2nd	3rd	total	%
1+	21	18	7	46	51.69
2+	17	16	9	42	47.19
17+	5	9	17	31	34.83
0+	13	8	2	23	25.84
3+	5	8	8	21	23.60
4+	10	4	3	17	19.10
5+	4	11	0	15	16.85
7+	4	2	7	13	14.61
12+	0	5	4	9	10.11
6+	2	2	4	8	8.99
16+	2	2	4	8	8.99
8+	4	1	2	7	7.87
9+	1	1	4	6	6.74
10+	1	0	3	4	4.49
11+	0	1	2	3	3.37
14+	0	1	2	3	3.37
13+	0	0	0	0	0.00
15+	0	0	0	0	0.00

Han Chases 4-7 runners (107)

odds	1st	2nd	3rd	total	%
2+	27	13	0	40	37.38
3+	19	21	0	40	37.38
4+	12	15	0	27	25.23
1+	13	10	0	23	21.50
6+	9	6	0	15	14.02
5+	3	11	0	14	13.08
7+	4	5	0	9	8.41
14+	3	5	0	8	7.48
8+	3	4	0	7	6.54
12+	2	5	0	7	6.54
0+	6	0	0	6	5.61
9+	1	2	1	4	3.74
10+	2	1	0	3	2.80
11+	1	1	0	2	1.87
17+	2	0	0	2	1.87
16+	0	1	0	1	0.93
13+	0	0	0	0	0.00
15+	0	0	0	0	0.00

Han Chases 8-11 runners (101)

odds	1st	2nd	3rd	total	%
4+	15	12	15	42	41.58
3+	12	16	10	38	37.62
7+	15	9	8	32	31.68
8+	8	9	9	26	25.74
2+	11	7	6	24	23.76
5+	12	7	3	22	21.78
6+	7	11	4	22	21.78
10+	5	10	6	21	20.79
12+	3	5	3	11	10.89
14+	1	2	7	10	9.90
16+	3	4	3	10	9.90
17+	2	2	6	10	9.90
1+	3	1	5	9	8.91
9+	3	2	2	7	6.93
11+	1	4	1	6	5.94
0+	0	0	0	0	0.00
13+	0	0	0	0	0.00
15+	0	0	0	0	0.00

Han Chases 12-15 runners (21)

odds	1st	2nd	3rd	total	%
10+	2	4	3	9	42.86
6+	3	3	1	7	33.33
4+	3	2	1	6	28.57
7+	2	1	2	5	23.81
17+	2	1	2	5	23.81
5+	2	0	2	4	19.05
9+	3	0	1	4	19.05
11+	2	1	1	4	19.05
2+	1	1	1	3	14.29
3+	0	1	2	3	14.29
8+	1	0	2	3	14.29
12+	0	2	1	3	14.29
14+	0	2	1	3	14.29
1+	0	2	0	2	9.52
16+	0	1	1	2	9.52
0+	0	0	0	0	0.00
13+	0	0	0	0	0.00
15+	0	0	0	0	0.00

Non Han Chases 4-7 runners (41)

odds	1st	2nd	3rd	total	%
0+	15	2	0	17	41.46
1+	10	5	0	15	36.59
3+	6	5	0	11	26.83
2+	5	4	0	9	21.95
4+	1	2	0	3	7.32
5+	2	1	0	3	7.32
17+	0	3	0	3	7.32
8+	0	2	0	2	4.88
10+	1	1	0	2	4.88
6+	0	1	0	1	2.44
7+	0	1	0	1	2.44
9+	0	1	0	1	2.44
12+	0	1	0	1	2.44
14+	1	0	0	1	2.44
11+	0	0	0	0	0.00
13+	0	0	0	0	0.00
15+	0	0	0	0	0.00
16+	0	0	0	0	0.00

Han All Weather 4-7 runners (62)

odds	1st	2nd	3rd	total	%
2+	14	12	0	26	41.94
1+	12	8	0	20	32.26
3+	9	4	0	13	20.97
5+	4	7	0	11	17.74
4+	4	5	1	10	16.13
0+	8	0	0	8	12.90
8+	3	4	0	7	11.29
12+	2	4	0	6	9.68
6+	2	3	0	5	8.06
7+	0	4	1	5	8.06
17+	1	3	0	4	6.45
16+	2	1	0	3	4.84
9+	0	2	0	2	3.23
10+	1	1	0	2	3.23
11+	0	1	0	1	1.61
13+	0	0	0	0	0.00
14+	0	0	0	0	0.00
15+	0	0	0	0	0.00

Non Han All Weather 12-15 runners (24)

odds	1st	2nd	3rd	total	%
2+	5	3	2	10	41.67
17+	0	6	4	10	41.67
5+	1	1	5	7	29.17
1+	3	1	2	6	25.00
3+	4	1	1	6	25.00
4+	1	1	2	4	16.67
8+	2	1	1	4	16.67
9+	1	1	2	4	16.67
12+	0	4	0	4	16.67
16+	2	2	0	4	16.67
0+	1	2	0	3	12.50
7+	1	1	1	3	12.50
6+	0	0	2	2	8.33
10+	1	0	1	2	8.33
14+	2	0	0	2	8.33
11+	0	0	1	1	4.17
13+	0	0	0	0	0.00
15+	0	0	0	0	0.00

Han Flat 4-7 runners (311)

odds	1st	2nd	3rd	total	%
2+	68	62	0	130	41.80
3+	52	52	0	104	33.44
1+	56	37	0	93	29.90
4+	33	32	0	65	20.90
5+	22	19	0	41	13.18
8+	18	17	0	35	11.25
0+	22	2	0	24	7.72
7+	9	15	0	24	7.72
6+	8	10	0	18	5.79
9+	4	7	0	11	3.54
12+	4	7	0	11	3.54
17+	3	7	0	10	3.22
10+	4	4	0	8	2.57
14+	6	2	0	8	2.57
16+	2	5	0	7	2.25
11+	0	4	0	4	1.29
13+	0	0	0	0	0.00
15+	0	0	0	0	0.00

Han Flat 8-11 runners (563)

odds	1st	2nd	3rd	total	%
4+	80	71	45	196	34.81
2+	103	60	32	195	34.64
3+	63	73	50	186	33.04
8+	40	55	55	150	26.64
5+	54	47	38	139	24.69
7+	37	37	42	116	20.60
6+	33	40	39	112	19.89
17+	24	37	40	101	17.94
1+	44	27	12	83	14.74
10+	23	32	26	81	14.39
12+	18	19	38	75	13.32
9+	7	21	16	44	7.82
14+	11	19	13	43	7.64
16+	11	11	15	37	6.57
11+	10	10	9	29	5.15
0+	5	4	0	9	1.60
13+	0	0	0	0	0.00
15+	0	0	0	0	0.00

Han Flat 12-15 runners (166)

odds	1st	2nd	3rd	total	%
17+	21	20	21	62	37.35
4+	18	28	12	58	34.94
8+	14	14	23	51	30.72
5+	20	12	11	43	25.90
12+	13	11	16	40	24.10
3+	9	15	14	38	22.89
6+	11	9	12	32	19.28
16+	8	11	13	32	19.28
10+	10	12	7	29	17.47
2+	13	10	3	26	15.66
7+	11	5	9	25	15.06
14+	6	4	15	25	15.06
9+	4	7	5	16	9.64
11+	3	5	3	11	6.63
1+	3	2	2	7	4.22
0+	2	1	0	3	1.81
13+	0	0	0	0	0.00
15+	0	0	0	0	0.00

Han Flat 16+ runners (56)

odds	1st	2nd	3rd	total	%
17+	7	7	17	31	55.36
8+	6	8	3	17	30.36
10+	6	5	6	17	30.36
14+	3	10	3	16	28.57
16+	8	5	3	16	28.57
7+	3	2	8	13	23.21
5+	8	2	2	12	21.43
4+	3	5	3	11	19.64
12+	2	4	5	11	19.64
9+	4	3	1	8	14.29
6+	4	1	1	6	10.71
11+	1	0	3	4	7.14
1+	0	2	0	2	3.57
2+	1	1	0	2	3.57
3+	0	1	1	2	3.57
0+	0	0	0	0	0.00
13+	0	0	0	0	0.00
15+	0	0	0	0	0.00

Non Han Flat 4-7 runners (198)

odds	1st	2nd	3rd	total	%
1+	47	22	0	69	34.85
0+	57	11	0	68	34.34
2+	29	34	0	63	31.82
3+	14	21	0	35	17.68
4+	12	19	0	31	15.66
5+	10	7	0	17	8.59
7+	4	13	0	17	8.59
6+	3	10	0	13	6.57
8+	6	6	0	12	6.06
17+	4	8	0	12	6.06
9+	2	5	0	7	3.54
10+	3	3	0	6	3.03
16+	2	4	0	6	3.03
11+	2	2	0	4	2.02
12+	3	1	0	4	2.02
14+	0	4	0	4	2.02
13+	0	0	0	0	0.00
15+	0	0	0	0	0.00

Non Han Flat 8-11 runners (246)

odds	1st	2nd	3rd	total	%
2+	36	32	25	93	37.80
1+	44	29	17	90	36.59
3+	33	27	24	84	34.15
4+	31	27	17	75	30.49
17+	10	19	35	64	26.02
7+	11	18	16	45	18.29
5+	16	14	14	44	17.89
0+	26	12	2	40	16.26
8+	6	15	11	32	13.01
10+	5	15	8	28	11.38
6+	5	7	11	23	9.35
12+	7	7	7	21	8.54
14+	8	5	7	20	8.13
16+	1	10	8	19	7.72
9+	3	5	9	17	6.91
11+	4	4	3	11	4.47
13+	0	0	0	0	0.00
15+	0	0	0	0	0.00

Non Han Flat 12-15 runners (100)

odds	1st	2nd	3rd	total	%
17+	8	16	17	41	41.00
1+	22	9	6	37	37.00
3+	13	3	12	28	28.00
2+	6	13	5	24	24.00
7+	7	5	11	23	23.00
4+	8	8	6	22	22.00
6+	5	7	7	19	19.00
8+	4	6	8	18	18.00
5+	6	7	4	17	17.00
14+	5	8	1	14	14.00
10+	3	4	6	13	13.00
12+	5	1	6	12	12.00
16+	1	6	5	12	12.00
0+	4	4	1	9	9.00
9+	0	3	3	6	6.00
11+	3	0	2	5	5.00
13+	0	0	0	0	0.00
15+	0	0	0	0	0.00

Non Han Flat 16+ runners (19)

odds	1st	2nd	3rd	total	%
17+	2	3	4	9	47.37
8+	2	0	4	6	31.58
16+	3	2	1	6	31.58
3+	0	3	2	5	26.32
5+	3	1	1	5	26.32
12+	1	1	3	5	26.32
4+	1	1	2	4	21.05
6+	1	2	1	4	21.05
14+	1	1	1	3	15.79
1+	1	1	0	2	10.53
7+	1	1	0	2	10.53
9+	0	2	0	2	10.53
10+	2	0	0	2	10.53
2+	1	0	0	1	5.26
11+	0	1	0	1	5.26
0+	0	0	0	0	0.00
13+	0	0	0	0	0.00
15+	0	0	0	0	0.00

TOP TWENTY PERCENTAGES RESULTS WIN AND PLACE by RACE TYPE

TYPE	ODDS	%
hf4	17+	55.36
nh2	1+	51.69
naw1	1+	51.16
nf4	17+	47.37
nh2	2+	47.19
nh1	0+	44.93
hch3	10+	42.86
haw1	2+	41.94
hf1	2+	41.8
naw3	2+	41.67
naw3	17+	41.67
hch2	4+	41.58
nch1	0+	41.46
nf3	17+	41
haw2	2+	40.96
nh1	2+	40.58
naw2	1+	40.54
hh1	2+	40
haw3	4+	40
naw2	2+	39.19

TOP TEN RESULTS of ODDS - ODDS/ON (0+) WIN and PLACE

TYPE	ODDS	%
nh1	0+	44.93
nch1	0+	41.46
nf1	0+	34.34
naw1	0+	27.91
nh2	0+	25.84
naw2	0+	25.68
nf2	0+	16.26
haw1	0+	12.9
naw3	0+	12.5
nf3	0+	9

TOP 10 RESULTS ODDS of 5+ WIN and PLACED

TYPE	ODDS	%
haw3	5+	30
naw3	5+	29.17
hh2	5+	29.1
nf4	5+	26.32
hh3	5+	25.93
haw2	5+	25.9
hf3	5+	25.9
hf2	5+	24.69
hch2	5+	21.78
hf4	5+	21.43

TOP 10 RESULTS ODDS of 10+ WIN and PLACED

TYPE	ODDS	%
hch3	10+	42.86
hf4	10+	30.36
hch2	10+	20.79
hf3	10+	17.47
haw3	10+	15
hf2	10+	14.39
hh2	10+	14.18
haw2	10+	13.86
nf3	10+	13
naw2	10+	12.16

TOP 10 RESULTS ODDS of 16+ WIN and PLACED

TYPE	ODDS	%
nf4	16+	31.58
hf4	16+	28.57
hh3	16+	27.78
hf3	16+	19.28
haw3	16+	18.75
naw3	16+	16.67
haw2	16+	15.06
nf3	16+	12
naw2	16+	10.81
hch2	16+	9.9

TOP 10 ODDS of 17+ WIN AND PLACE

TYPE	ODDS	%
hf4	17+	55.36
nf4	17+	47.37
naw3	17+	41.67
nf3	17+	41
hf3	17+	37.35
nh2	17+	34.83
naw2	17+	31.08
hh3	17+	27.78
haw3	17+	27.5
nf2	17+	26.02

PART TWO WIN ONLY

In this section I have used the same statistics as before but using only the win results. You will see in the following tables I have just used the column headed 1st showing the time the number of horses with the odds denoted in the first column have won.

Han Hurdles 4-7 runners (50)

odds	1st	%
2+	13	26.00
4+	7	14.00
1+	6	12.00
3+	5	10.00
5+	5	10.00
0+	3	6.00
6+	3	6.00
7+	2	4.00
8+	2	4.00
9+	1	2.00
10+	1	2.00
12+	1	2.00
14+	1	2.00
11+	0	0.00
13+	0	0.00
15+	0	0.00
16+	0	0.00
17+	0	0.00

Han Hurdles 8-11 runners (134)

odds	1st	%
3+	20	14.93
2+	18	13.43
4+	17	12.69
5+	16	11.94
6+	12	8.96
1+	11	8.21
7+	8	5.97
8+	6	4.48
12+	6	4.48
0+	5	3.73
10+	5	3.73
17+	4	2.99
9+	3	2.24
14+	2	1.49
16+	1	0.75
11+	0	0.00
13+	0	0.00
15+	0	0.00

Han Hurdles 12-15 runners (54)

odds	1st	%
9+	7	12.96
2+	6	11.11
3+	6	11.11
16+	6	11.11
5+	4	7.41
6+	4	7.41
8+	4	7.41
4+	3	5.56
7+	3	5.56
12+	3	5.56
17+	3	5.56
1+	2	3.70
11+	2	3.70
14+	1	1.85
0+	0	0.00
10+	0	0.00
13+	0	0.00
15+	0	0.00

Non Han Hurdles 4-7 runners (69)

odds	1st	%
0+	22	31.88
2+	15	21.74
1+	13	18.84
3+	5	7.25
4+	5	7.25
10+	2	2.90
17+	2	2.90
5+	1	1.45
8+	1	1.45
9+	1	1.45
11+	1	1.45
12+	1	1.45
6+	0	0.00
7+	0	0.00
13+	0	0.00
14+	0	0.00
15+	0	0.00
16+	0	0.00

Non Han Hurdles 8-11 runners (89)

odds	1st	%
1+	21	23.60
2+	17	19.10
0+	13	14.61
4+	10	11.24
3+	5	5.62
17+	5	5.62
5+	4	4.49
7+	4	4.49
8+	4	4.49
6+	2	2.25
16+	2	2.25
9+	1	1.12
10+	1	1.12
11+	0	0.00
12+	0	0.00
13+	0	0.00
14+	0	0.00
15+	0	0.00

Han Chases 4-7 runners (107)

odds	1st	%
2+	27	25.23
3+	19	17.76
1+	13	12.15
4+	12	11.21
6+	9	8.41
0+	6	5.61
7+	4	3.74
5+	3	2.80
8+	3	2.80
14+	3	2.80
10+	2	1.87
12+	2	1.87
17+	2	1.87
9+	1	0.93
11+	1	0.93
13+	0	0.00
15+	0	0.00
16+	0	0.00

Han Chases 8-11 runners (101)

odds	1st	%
4+	15	14.85
7+	15	14.85
3+	12	11.88
5+	12	11.88
2+	11	10.89
8+	8	7.92
6+	7	6.93
10+	5	4.95
1+	3	2.97
9+	3	2.97
12+	3	2.97
16+	3	2.97
17+	2	1.98
11+	1	0.99
14+	1	0.99
0+	0	0.00
13+	0	0.00
15+	0	0.00

Han Chases 12-15 runners (21)

odds	1st	%
4+	3	14.29
6+	3	14.29
9+	3	14.29
5+	2	9.52
7+	2	9.52
10+	2	9.52
11+	2	9.52
17+	2	9.52
2+	1	4.76
8+	1	4.76
0+	0	0.00
1+	0	0.00
3+	0	0.00
12+	0	0.00
13+	0	0.00
14+	0	0.00
15+	0	0.00
16+	0	0.00

Non Han Chases 4-7 runners (41)

odds	1st	%
0+	15	36.59
1+	10	24.39
3+	6	14.63
2+	5	12.20
5+	2	4.88
4+	1	2.44
10+	1	2.44
14+	1	2.44
6+	0	0.00
7+	0	0.00
8+	0	0.00
9+	0	0.00
11+	0	0.00
12+	0	0.00
13+	0	0.00
15+	0	0.00
16+	0	0.00
17+	0	0.00

Han All Weather 4-7 runners (62)

odds	1st	%
2+	14	22.58
1+	12	19.35
3+	9	14.52
0+	8	12.90
4+	4	6.45
5+	4	6.45
8+	3	4.84
6+	2	3.23
12+	2	3.23
16+	2	3.23
10+	1	1.61
17+	1	1.61
7+	0	0.00
9+	0	0.00
11+	0	0.00
13+	0	0.00
14+	0	0.00
15+	0	0.00

Han All Weather 8-11 runners (166)

odds	1st	%
2+	31	18.67
3+	27	16.27
1+	23	13.86
5+	10	6.02
7+	10	6.02
8+	10	6.02
16+	10	6.02
0+	9	5.42
4+	9	5.42
10+	8	4.82
6+	4	2.41
9+	4	2.41
11+	4	2.41
17+	4	2.41
14+	3	1.81
12+	0	0.00
13+	0	0.00
15+	0	0.00

Han All Weather 12-15 runners (80)

odds	1st	%
3+	11	13.75
5+	11	13.75
4+	10	12.50
1+	7	8.75
2+	7	8.75
16+	6	7.50
8+	5	6.25
6+	4	5.00
7+	4	5.00
9+	4	5.00
12+	3	3.75
17+	3	3.75
11+	2	2.50
0+	1	1.25
10+	1	1.25
14+	1	1.25
13+	0	0.00
15+	0	0.00

Non Han All Weather 4-7 runners (43)

odds	1st	%
1+	14	32.56
0+	11	25.58
2+	11	25.58
3+	3	6.98
4+	1	2.33
10+	1	2.33
14+	1	2.33
17+	1	2.33
5+	0	0.00
6+	0	0.00
7+	0	0.00
8+	0	0.00
9+	0	0.00
11+	0	0.00
12+	0	0.00
13+	0	0.00
15+	0	0.00
16+	0	0.00

Non Han All Weather 8-11 runners (74)

odds	1st	%
1+	16	21.62
0+	13	17.57
2+	10	13.51
4+	7	9.46
17+	7	9.46
3+	4	5.41
7+	4	5.41
6+	3	4.05
10+	3	4.05
5+	2	2.70
12+	2	2.70
16+	2	2.70
8+	1	1.35
9+	0	0.00
11+	0	0.00
13+	0	0.00
14+	0	0.00
15+	0	0.00

Non Han All Weather 12-11 runners (24)

odds	1st	%
2+	5	20.83
3+	4	16.67
1+	3	12.50
8+	2	8.33
14+	2	8.33
16+	2	8.33
0+	1	4.17
4+	1	4.17
5+	1	4.17
7+	1	4.17
9+	1	4.17
10+	1	4.17
6+	0	0.00
11+	0	0.00
12+	0	0.00
13+	0	0.00
15+	0	0.00
17+	0	0.00

Han Flat 4-7 runners (311)

odds	1st	%
2+	68	21.86
1+	56	18.01
3+	52	16.72
4+	33	10.61
0+	22	7.07
5+	22	7.07
8+	18	5.79
7+	9	2.89
6+	8	2.57
14+	6	1.93
9+	4	1.29
10+	4	1.29
12+	4	1.29
17+	3	0.96
16+	2	0.64
11+	0	0.00
13+	0	0.00
15+	0	0.00

Han Flat 8-11 runners (563)

odds	1st	%
2+	103	18.29
4+	80	14.21
3+	63	11.19
5+	54	9.59
1+	44	7.82
8+	40	7.10
7+	37	6.57
6+	33	5.86
17+	24	4.26
10+	23	4.09
12+	18	3.20
14+	11	1.95
16+	11	1.95
11+	10	1.78
9+	7	1.24
0+	5	0.89
13+	0	0.00
15+	0	0.00

Han Flat 12-15 runners (166)

odds	1st	%
17+	21	12.65
5+	20	12.05
4+	18	10.84
8+	14	8.43
2+	13	7.83
12+	13	7.83
6+	11	6.63
7+	11	6.63
10+	10	6.02
3+	9	5.42
16+	8	4.82
14+	6	3.61
9+	4	2.41
1+	3	1.81
11+	3	1.81
0+	2	1.20
13+	0	0.00
15+	0	0.00

Han Flat 16+ runners (56)

odds	1st	%
5+	8	14.29
16+	8	14.29
17+	7	12.50
8+	6	10.71
10+	6	10.71
6+	4	7.14
9+	4	7.14
4+	3	5.36
7+	3	5.36
14+	3	5.36
12+	2	3.57
2+	1	1.79
11+	1	1.79
0+	0	0.00
1+	0	0.00
3+	0	0.00
13+	0	0.00
15+	0	0.00

Non Han Flat 4-7 runners (198)

odds	1st	%
0+	57	28.79
1+	47	23.74
2+	29	14.65
3+	14	7.07
4+	12	6.06
5+	10	5.05
8+	6	3.03
7+	4	2.02
17+	4	2.02
6+	3	1.52
10+	3	1.52
12+	3	1.52
9+	2	1.01
11+	2	1.01
16+	2	1.01
13+	0	0.00
14+	0	0.00
15+	0	0.00

Non Han Flat 8-11 runners (246)

odds	1st	%
1+	44	17.89
2+	36	14.63
3+	33	13.41
4+	31	12.60
0+	26	10.57
5+	16	6.50
7+	11	4.47
17+	10	4.07
14+	8	3.25
12+	7	2.85
8+	6	2.44
6+	5	2.03
10+	5	2.03
11+	4	1.63
9+	3	1.22
16+	1	0.41
13+	0	0.00
15+	0	0.00

Non Han Flat 12-15 runners (100)

odds	1st	%
1+	44	17.89
2+	36	14.63
3+	33	13.41
4+	31	12.60
0+	26	10.57
5+	16	6.50
7+	11	4.47
17+	10	4.07
14+	8	3.25
12+	7	2.85
8+	6	2.44
6+	5	2.03
10+	5	2.03
11+	4	1.63
9+	3	1.22
16+	1	0.41
13+	0	0.00
15+	0	0.00

Non Han Flat 16+ runners (19)

odds	1st	%
5+	3	15.79
16+	3	15.79
8+	2	10.53
10+	2	10.53
17+	2	10.53
1+	1	5.26
2+	1	5.26
4+	1	5.26
6+	1	5.26
7+	1	5.26
12+	1	5.26
14+	1	5.26
0+	0	0.00
3+	0	0.00
9+	0	0.00
11+	0	0.00
13+	0	0.00
15+	0	0.00

BEST PERCENTAGES for WIN by RACE TYPE

	odds	%
nch1	0+	36.59
naw1	1+	32.56
nh1	0+	31.88
nf1	0+	28.79
hh1	2+	26
naw1	0+	25.58
naw1	2+	25.58
hch1	2+	25.23
nch1	1+	24.39
nf1	1+	23.74
nh2	1+	23.6
haw1	2+	22.58
nf3	1+	22
hf1	2+	21.86
nh1	2+	21.74
naw2	1+	21.62
naw3	2+	20.83
haw1	1+	19.35
nh2	2+	19.1
nh1	1+	18.84

TOP 10 ODDS ON (0+) WIN ONLY

TYPE	ODDS	%
nch1	0+	36.59
nh1	0+	31.88
nf1	0+	28.79
naw1	0+	25.58
naw2	0+	17.57
nh2	0+	14.61
haw1	0+	12.9
nf2	0+	10.57
hf1	0+	7.07
hh1	0+	6

TOP 10 ODDS of 5+ WIN ONLY

TYPE	ODDS	%
nf4	5+	15.79
hf4	5+	14.29
haw3	5+	13.75
hf3	5+	12.05
hh2	5+	11.94
hch2	5+	11.88
hh1	5+	10
hf2	5+	9.59
hch3	5+	9.52
hh3	5+	7.41

TOP 10 ODDS of 10+ WIN ONLY

TYPE	ODDS	%
hf4	10+	10.71
nf4	10+	10.53
hch3	10+	9.52
hf3	10+	6.02
hch2	10+	4.95
haw2	10+	4.82
naw3	10+	4.17
hf2	10+	4.09
naw2	10+	4.05
hh2	10+	3.73

TOP 10 ODDS of 16+ WIN ONLY

TYPE	ODDS	%
nf4	16+	15.79
hf4	16+	14.29
hh3	16+	11.11
naw3	16+	8.33
haw3	16+	7.5
haw2	16+	6.02
hf3	16+	4.82
haw1	16+	3.23
hch2	16+	2.97
naw2	16+	2.7

TOP TEN ODDS of 17+ WIN ONLY

TYPE	ODDS	%
hf3	17+	12.65
hf4	17+	12.5
nf4	17+	10.53
hch3	17+	9.52
naw2	17+	9.46
nf3	17+	8
nh2	17+	5.62
hh3	17+	5.56
hf2	17+	4.26
nf2	17+	4.07

SUMMERY

I have tried to keep the book small and easy to follow; it's not easy with this type of book. Lots of tables to compile and I understand it can be a bit of a labor to follow them. I hope this is not the case. All the work has been done using excel work sheets by Microsoft. They are not prone to errors and I hope there is no error on my part. I do not mess with the results, they are printed as they come up once excel has done its work sorting the statistics into highest/ lowest, percentages etc.

This is my fourth book in the range; I try to compile statistics that you don't usually find around horse racing in the racing press or on-line. Jockey tables, trainer tables etc etc; there is a wealth of stuff out there but sometimes there are just some questions that are missed.

How much you will find this book useful or more importantly it helps you find some winners is hard for me to judge. Please do not bank on it as there is a lot to horse racing other than just the odds they return at. It is still flesh and blood horses with a human on top running through mud so it always a gamble.

Nevertheless I believe any help or information can lessen that gamble and I hope this proves the case with this book or any other of my books. However, I don't advise how you should gamble, I leave that completely up to the reader, I just compile the statistics and print them; I try to give as good a description what the book contains so no one buys the book and feels disappointed. If you are, I am sorry, I did my best.

I have three other books all titled "Horse Racing the Statistical Route" covering Form, The first 4 horses in the betting and Racing Post ratings for horses. I am looking at a 5th book just covering race card numbers which might be published soon depending on what I have.

Wishing you good luck and thanks for looking.

Contents

Horse Racing the Statistical Route Four 1
Purely Odds-Starting Prices Sp's of Horses 1
ABOUT THE BOOK 2
   THE BOOK LAYOUT 3
   NOTE: - Non Runners 5
      JUST A WARNING ABOUT STATISTICS 5
   WHERE THE ODDS FALL WIN AND PLACED 6
      Han Hurdles 4-7 runners (50) 7
      Han Hurdles 8-11 runners (134) 7
      Han Hurdles 12-15 runners (54) 8
      Non Han Hurdles 4-7 runners (69) 8
      Non Han Hurdles 8-11 runners (89) 9
      Han Chases 4-7 runners (107) 9
      Han Chases 8-11 runners (101) 10
      Han Chases 12-15 runners (21) 10
      Non Han Chases 4-7 runners (41) 11
      Han All Weather 4-7 runners (62) 11
      Han All Weather 8-11 runners (166) 12
      Han All Weather 12-15 runners (80) 12
      Non Han All Weather 4-7 runners (43) 13
      Non Han All Weather 8-11 runners (74) 13
      Non Han All Weather 12-15 runners (24) 14
      Han Flat 4-7 runners (311) 14
      Han Flat 8-11 runners (563) 15
      Han Flat 12-15 runners (166) 15
      Han Flat 16+ runners (56) 16
      Non Han Flat 4-7 runners (198) 16
      Non Han Flat 8-11 runners (246) 17
      Non Han Flat 12-15 runners (100) 17
      Non Han Flat 16+ runners (19) 18
   TOP TWENTY PERCENTAGES RESULTS WIN AND PLACE by RACE TYPE 19
   TOP TEN RESULTS of ODDS - ODDS/ON (0+) WIN and PLACE 20
   TOP 10 RESULTS ODDS of 5+ WIN and PLACED 20

TOP 10 RESULTS ODDS of 16+ WIN and PLACED	21
TOP 10 ODDS of 17+ WIN AND PLACE	22
PART TWO WIN ONLY	23
Han Hurdles 4-7 runners (50)	24
Han Hurdles 8-11 runners (134)	24
Han Hurdles 12-15 runners (54)	25
Non Han Hurdles 4-7 runners (69)	25
Non Han Hurdles 8-11 runners (89)	26
Han Chases 4-7 runners (107)	26
Han Chases 8-11 runners (101)	27
Han Chases 12-15 runners (21)	27
Non Han Chases 4-7 runners (41)	28
Han All Weather 4-7 runners (62)	28
Han All Weather 8-11 runners (166)	29
Han All Weather 12-15 runners (80)	29
Non Han All Weather 4-7 runners (43)	30
Non Han All Weather 8-11 runners (74)	30
Non Han All Weather 12-11 runners (24)	31
Han Flat 4-7 runners (311)	31
Han Flat 8-11 runners (563)	32
Han Flat 12-15 runners (166)	32
Han Flat 16+ runners (56)	33
Non Han Flat 4-7 runners (198)	33
Non Han Flat 8-11 runners (246)	34
Non Han Flat 12-15 runners (100)	34
Non Han Flat 16+ runners (19)	35
BEST PERCENTAGES for WIN by RACE TYPE	36
TOP 10 ODDS ON (0+) WIN ONLY	37
TOP 10 ODDS of 5+ WIN ONLY	37
TOP 10 ODDS of 10+ WIN ONLY	38
TOP 10 ODDS of 16+ WIN ONLY	38
TOP TEN ODDS of 17+ WIN ONLY	39
SUMMERY	40